The Needful Thing

TWENTY-ONE BIBLICAL **TRUTHS** TO REFRES**HER** SPIRIT

FELICIA D. SHELTON
FOREWORD BY PAUL E. SHELTON SR.

Cocoon to Wings
PUBLISHING

THE NEEDFUL THING

Printed in the United States of America
ISBN: 978-1-953497-67-3 (Hardcover)
ISBN: 978-1-953497-65-9 (Paperback)

Library of Congress Control Number: 2023911500

Published by Cocoon to Wings Publishing
7810 Gall Blvd., #311
Zephyrhills, FL 33541
www.CocoontoWingsBooks.com
(813) 906-WING (9464)

Book cover redesign by ETP Creative

The Needful Thing

TWENTY-ONE BIBLICAL **TRUTHS** TO REFRES**HER** SPIRIT

FELICIA D. SHELTON
FOREWORD BY PAUL E. SHELTON SR.

A Table of Words

She had a sister called Mary, who sat at the Lord's feet, listening to what He said.

Luke 10:39
New International Version (NIV)

Now it came to pass, as they went, that He entered a certain village: and a certain woman named Martha received Him into her house. And she had a sister called Mary, which also sat at Jesus's feet and heard His word. But Martha was cumbered about much serving and came to Him and said, "Lord, dost thou not care that my sister hath left me to serve alone? Bid her therefore that she help me." And Jesus answered and said unto her, "Martha, Martha, thou art careful and troubled about many things: But one thing is needful: and Mary hath chosen that good part, which shall not be taken away from her."

— Luke 10:38–42 (NIV)

Dedication

This book is dedicated to women who desire a deeper relationship with God, to women who are yearning for more of God's glory, to women who are devoted to stealing away daily to meet with God face-to-face, to women who long to be refreshed and renewed in their minds daily, to women who are committed to spending quality time in the secret place of the Most High God, to women who refuse to have a third-party relationship with God, to women who refuse to learn of God only by way of someone else's testimony, to women who are devoted to loving the world around them as God commands, and to women who are devoted to the Needful Thing.

Foreword

I would like to thank our Lord and Savior for giving Felicia Shelton the revelation, passion, and spiritual withal to write *The Needful Thing*. For more than twenty years, I have found Felicia to be a woman who loves God and His people. She has been found to be faithful to God and committed to spreading the good news. She is a devoted wife, mother, and friend, a woman truly on a mission to scatter love and the truth of God's Word everywhere she treads. God's good hand is truly upon her. God has graced Felicia to reveal the truth, significance, and power of the Needful Thing. On many occasions, I am approached by individuals who state to me, "You know, your wife is an incredible woman of God." Without hesitation or surprise, I simply reply, "Yes, she is." In all honesty, I am keenly aware of the anointing that rests heavily upon Felicia's life. Through her devotion to God, will to win, and spiritual fortitude, I know firsthand that she has paid the price for the anointing that rests on her life. I have never met a woman of God as loving, caring, and committed to the call of God on her life as Felicia. She is not only a hearer of the Word but also a doer, and she leads by example. I trust the Spirit of God that dwells within her, and even in moments when I do not fully understand what she is doing, I understand whom she is doing it for.

Felicia is very passionate about doing the will of God. She has a special grace in her life to minister to women and young ladies from various age groups and diverse walks of life. She is utterly determined to see God restore and refresh the lives of women who have been abused, abandoned, and ostracized by religious conditionings and societal norms as a consequence of their social statuses, genders, ethnicities, races, personal convictions, and God-inspired revelations. Felicia is also a woman of generosity. Having said that, I have had to pray without ceasing as well as be in tune with what God has led her to do for those in need, oftentimes praying that she does not give away the whole farm. For years, I have witnessed Felicia give her time, talents, and resources to women in need of spiritual guidance and natural resources. Equally significant, Felicia is convinced that the Needful Thing is the vehicle by which the broken are restored and refreshed.

In *The Needful Thing*, you will be inspired to draw nigh to God. As you continue forward reading *The Needful Thing*, you will be encouraged to steal away daily and sit at God's feet. When we spend time with God, alone in His secret place, something happens. I am certain spiritual refreshment will happen for you as you delve deeper into *The Needful Thing*. I am convinced that your spirit will be strengthened as you read *The Needful Thing*. I am also convinced that *The Needful Thing* will provoke you to hunger and thirst for more of God. And I am convinced that as you embrace the truths that are yet to be revealed in *The Needful Thing*, you will be refreshed. So, I welcome you to join Felicia as she reveals twenty-one biblical truths and revelations about what matters most in the life of every believer, to which is the Needful Thing.

PAUL EDWARD SHELTON SR.
PROUD HUSBAND

Preface

Now it came to pass, as they went, that He entered into a certain village: and a certain woman named Martha received Him into her house. And she had a sister called Mary, which also sat at Jesus's feet and heard His word. But Martha was cumbered about much serving and came to Him and said, "Lord, dost thou not care that my sister hath left me to serve alone? Bid her therefore that she help me." And Jesus answered and said unto her, "Martha, Martha, thou art careful and troubled about many things. But one thing is needful: and Mary hath chosen that good part, which shall not be taken away from her" (Luke 10:38–42, NIV).

The very nature of women, in many cases, is multifaceted and inundated with a myriad of tasks. The average woman wears various hats and serves in many capacities—daily, might I add. Oftentimes women are cumbered about much serving because of their loyalty and love for their families, local churches, communities, and friends. But the one thing above all that is most important in a woman's life, that brings with it great spiritual rewards, is what Christ referred to as the Needful Thing. The Needful Thing, as Mary discovered, was spending time with the Messiah. Today the Needful Thing in our lives is spending time with God in an up-close and personal way. The Needful Thing, although very rewarding, is oftentimes undervalued and replaced with busy work, busy lives, and personal prayers, which oftentimes are made known to God whenever we can fit Him into our busy schedules. But the Needful Thing encompasses so much more than communing with God on the run. The Needful Thing is about intentionally setting aside time daily to spend personal time alone with God.

Daily, God extends an open invitation to each of us to rest at His feet. The invitation to fellowship with God is one of the greatest honors Abba has bestowed upon every born-again believer. God has granted every believer direct access to commune with Him. Just as a mother longs to be close to her children, God longs to have more than a distant relationship with His children (Matthew 6:6, James 4:8, 1 John 1:3, John 15:1–5, Leviticus 26:12). God desires to commune with His children every single day of their lives. And God wants to have a deeper, more mature relationship with each of us. Spending time alone with God is more than a casual conversation or an act of duty; it is an opportunity as well as a privilege to get to know the almighty, all-knowing, loving, infinite God deeper. Moreover, God wants to spend quality time alone with us to refresh us spiritually. He wants to engage in conversation and fellowship with us to strengthen us, guide us into all truth, and meet our every need, but if we are too busy to pause our lives to steal away with Him, we will miss out on all the benefits that come with spending personal time alone with God.

As Christ proclaims in Luke 10:42, "There is only one thing worth being concerned about," and Mary portrayed the very essence of this truth. Mary understood long before her sister Martha that the Needful Thing was spending time at the Messiah's feet. The Needful Thing was not being cumbered about much serving. Of a truth, the most Needful Thing in a believer's life is constant fellowship with God. It is needful for believers to lie at God's feet and commune with Him daily without interruption or distraction. It is needful for believers to steal away daily from the hustle and bustle of life to spend time with the Father. And it is needful for followers of Christ to know God in an up-close and personal way. In summation, times of refreshing come from spending time in the presence of God (Acts 3:19).

In more cases than not, the busyness of life, personal endeavors, career aspirations, educational pursuits, and ministry commitments within church walls impede upon believers' ability to steal away daily to spend quality time with God, but steal away, we must, as spending time at the feet of God is not an option. It is a necessary ingredient that determines a believer's capacity to love without constraints, remain steadfast in faith, forgive those who have trespassed against them, live a victorious life, and remain refreshed in their spirits. As noted in Luke 10:38–42, Martha's busyness was a distraction, but Mary discovered the Needful Thing. She understood the importance of kneeling at Yeshua's (Deliverer, Savior) feet. She understood that worship at Christ's feet would renew her spirit, raise her knowledge of Him, and refresh her troubled soul. The same rings true for women of God today. The Needful Thing in the life of every Godly woman is daily communion with God.

As you study God's sacred Word, meditate on the ensuing biblical truths penned in this devotional, and make it a daily priority to spend time alone with God, I am convinced that your mind will be renewed, your spirit will be refreshed, your capacity to love as God commands will increase, and your faith will be fortified. The confidence I have in knowing the benefits of spending time alone with God stems from a personal relationship I have developed with God through spending time alone with Him consistently. Despite any success, victory, test, or obstacle that has come to challenge my faith or trouble my soul, during times like these, I have always found peace, restoration, strength, and spiritual refreshment from spending time with God.

Thanks to So Many

A heartfelt thank you to Yeshua Hamashiach (Anointed one), the one who appoints us, anoints us, leads us, and carries us through every test, trial, and victory. Thanks to Holy Spirit, our comforter and loyal guide.

A heartfelt, eternal thank you to my beloved mother, my lifelong role model and shero, Delores Isham-Presley, who faithfully modeled the characteristics of Christ before me, and taught me at an early age the significance of surrendering my life to Christ as well as caring for those in need.

In addition, I wish to thank my loving husband, soulmate, and best friend, Paul Edward Shelton Sr., for supporting me throughout this mission and for lending me his Godly wisdom and counsel when I needed it most. I love you eternally.

Thanks to my children, whom I love more than words could ever convey—Aubrianna, Kiyah, and Paul Jr. You are my true joy and motivation.

A heartfelt thank you to my sister and friend, Francitta V. Williams, for always lending me her creative thoughts, expertise, and time. Thank you from the bottom of my heart for designing the cover of this manuscript in the spirit of excellence and sisterly love. Your labor of love is highly appreciated.

And thanks to my family and spiritual sisters who prayed for me, encouraged me, and cheered for me while this mission and its editing processes were underway. I love each of you dearly.

Summary

The Needful Thing is a devotional guide for women that is founded on Luke 10:38–42. In *The Needful Thing*, twenty-one biblical truths are revealed to emphasize what is most needful in every woman's life. This devotional will provide contemplative meditations that are practical and meaningful. It is designed to help women maintain, claim, and discover times of spiritual refreshment, peace, and joy. Written within this manuscript are five bite-size devotionals, entitled *Times of Refreshing: Mission Possible, A Lamp and a Light Word Feast, Morning Manna Bites, A Command to Love*, and Her*story: Daily Devotional Letters to Inspire Her Heart*, and seven bite-size prayers, entitled "Help Me to Love as Thou Commands," "A Prayer of Thanksgiving," "A Prayer for the Lost," "A Prayer of Refreshing," "My Sister's Keeper Prayer," "A Prayer of Confidence and Faith," and "A Prayer for Rest." These fundamental commentaries are designed to help women build a deeper, more mature relationship with God. These writings can be used daily while spending time with God.

In *Times of Refreshing: Mission Possible*, women will be reminded of key elements that lead to a refreshed life. This chapter will admonish women to commit to a lifestyle of fellowship with God, which entails spending personal time in the presence of God.

In *A Lamp and a Light Word Feast*, women will be invited to feast off and meditate on key passages for seven consecutive days. The foundational Scripture for this time of devotion is Psalm 119:105 (KJV).

In *Morning Manna Bites*, bite-size devotions are provided for women to delve into the Word of God. The real-life accounts of the author are shared as a means by which she uses her personal testimonies to bring to life the correlation between Scripture and modern daily living.

In *A Command to Love*, 1 Corinthians 13 is the foundational text used to bring to life the true essence of love. This commentary provides a portrait of love and encourages readers to model the attributes of love as noted in this passage. Readers are reminded that everything hinges on love and that love is a very vital key to spiritual freedom and refreshment.

In Her*story: Daily Devotional Letters to Inspire Her Heart*, love letters written by the author are shared to provoke women to walk in the way of love as God commands. These writings are real-life accounts experienced by the author. The primary focus of these letters is to emphasize the significance and power of love. Each day during this period, a "love charge" is suggested to provoke women to employ specific acts of love throughout the course of their daily lives and beyond. Devotional Scriptures are also provided as points of biblical references for women to meditate on and act upon throughout their daily tasks and interactions with others.

In *Bite-Size Prayers*, women are encouraged to pray without ceasing. Seven specific prayer topics are provided for readers to incorporate in their daily time of prayer and communion with God.

TIMES OF REFRESHING: MISSION POSSIBLE

If you desire spiritual refreshment, if you are longing for more of God, if you are yearning for constant rivers of living water to flow in your life, and if you are tired of busy work that consumes you to the point that you rarely have time to spend alone with God, this book is for you. Through the ensuing writings, you will be invited to journey to a place that leads to spiritual renewal and strength, a place that leads you deeper into the presence of God. According to the *Merriam-Webster Dictionary*, to be refreshed means "to restore strength and animation, to revive, to replenish, to freshen up, [to] renovate." Penned within the subsequent pages are fundamental truths designed to help you realize the Needful Thing, which has a great propensity to revive, replenish, renovate, and freshen your mind, spirit, and soul. As denoted in Acts 3:20, times of refreshing come from time spent in the presence of God (NIV). Mary understood the significance of this truth. She understood that being a busy body would distract her from spending quality time with the Messiah. Just as Mary understood this essential truth, it is needful for every woman of God to pursue and act upon this truth daily.

The journey to spiritual refreshment calls for one to live a lifestyle of sincere devotion and fellowship with God. Believers who seek God's face daily as well as spend personal time alone with Him will realize spiritual refreshment. The journey to living a continual refreshed life, however, begins with making a conscious decision to commune with God daily. I encourage you to make it a way of life to begin each day with a heart of gratitude and meditation on God's love, goodness, and faithfulness before any other thoughts or incidents gain entrance into your thought processes. Personally, I have found that early-morning meditation and fellowship with God helps set the tone for the rest of the day. Even greater, Abba desires to refresh us daily. Abba desires to commune with us face-to-face. Abba desires to build a personal relationship with us that transcends beyond church walls, religious events, or third-party relationships, relationships that are built on someone else's testimony, sermon, or insight rather than a personal encounter with God.

Think on this for a moment: God desires to spend time with you. How amazing and heartwarming is it to know this very truth? Knowing this truth touches my heart in ways that are unexplainable. When I think of the fact that our Holy Supreme God desires to spend time with me, it moves me to an overwhelming place of gratitude and appreciation. But it also moves me to respond in a way that reciprocates the same sentiments back to God. I too long to spend time with God. For years, I have been moved to respond in a way that compels me to dedicate time each day to meet with God and tell Him just how much I love Him, need Him. To bear good fruit for God's glory, it is needful to spend time in His presence and remain in a place of gratitude and thanksgiving. My hope and prayer for you is that you would accept God's invitation to steal away with Him daily and rest at His feet.

Times of Refreshing: Mission Possible

INVITATION

The very peace of mind we long for each day is found in the presence of God. Our heavenly Father provides everything we need. I encourage you to be intentional about carving out a time and distinct place to commune with God daily. With a gentle nudge and kind gesture, I invite you to open your heart to the subsequent biblical truths. Equally, as you form a fellowship with God each day, enter His presence with a repenting heart and an open heart to receive what He has in store for you. As He speaks to you, be willing to change old mind-sets and ways of doing things. Throughout your spiritual journey, as you progress further and further into God's glory, He will speak to you concerning old attitudes, mind-sets, and offenses. Be open. God sees all and knows all. He knows what is best for you. As you open your heart to Him, He will show you all that is needed to prepare you for greater levels of spiritual refreshment.

Of equal significance, I invite you to meditate on God's goodness and praise Him for all that He has done in your life. Make your request known unto Him and be sure to wait patiently before Him to h*ear* (*may your spiritual ears be opened*) what He has to say to you. He that has an ear, let him hear what the Spirit has to say to the churches (Revelations 3:6). Be sure to listen, expecting to h*ear* God's voice. I promise you, as you wait patiently before Him and anticipate an encounter with Him, He will answer you and reveal to you great and mighty things (Jeremiah 3:33). Moreover, as you seek God daily, I invite you to make a conscious effort to devote time in Bible reading. God's Word is a source of refreshment to the believer's soul. When we draw near God, our minds are renewed, and our spirits are refreshed.

Mary chose to spend time at Yeshua's feet and increase her knowledge of Him. Martha chose otherwise. Martha was so busy working to serve Yeshua that she did not have time to sit at His feet. She did not have time to get to know Him deeper. As noted in Scripture, Martha chose work over worship; this decision caused her to be troubled rather than refreshed. Like many among Yeshua's followers today, work within and outside church walls takes precedence over spending personal time with God. This way of living is at an all-time high, and there is indeed a price to pay for choosing work over time spent with God. There must be an equal balance between spending personal time alone with God and working for Him as one should not be sacrificed for the other. In more cases than not, the lack of building a personal relationship with God in exchange for working diligently for God leads to spiritual burnout and discouragement. Please lend me a moment to state that "I am a proponent of working within church walls as long as it is for His glory," but what we do for God should never be at the expense of getting to know Him personally or spending quality time alone with Him.

Therefore, I urge you to prioritize spending time daily with God. And I urge you to choose to quiet your heart every day to rest at His feet so that you may experience deeper encounters with Him. It is my sincere hope that just as Mary discovered and embraced the Needful Thing, the same will ring true for you for the rest of your days here on Earth.

A LAMP AND A
LIGHT FEAST

> *Thy word is a lamp unto my feet and a light unto my path.*
> — Psalm 119:105 (KJV)

"O taste and see that the Lord is good!" (Psalm 34:8). The Word of God is a necessary ingredient in a righteous woman's life. It is the divine source of spiritual nutrients that helps women maintain spiritual insight, Godly wisdom, and spiritual prowess. Daily consumption of the Word of God is paramount to building a relationship with God. Nothing compares to the feast of love and refreshment found in spending time with God through sacred Scripture.

As the psalmist declares, the Word of God is good because it helps us see more vividly the path God has for us to travel. It is a lamp unto our feet and a light unto our paths (Psalm 119:105). One of the ways we find strength for the journey ahead is through digesting the sacred Word of God. It is needful for God-fearing women to feast off the Word of God and spend time in His presence daily. Digesting the Word of God keeps our relationships with God fresh and renews our faith (Acts 3:20; Romans 10:17).

Over the next seven days, as you feast off the ensuing Scriptures, may God's Word be a lamp unto your feet and a light unto your path. May He lead you into deeper levels of spiritual strength and refreshment. I gently urge you to quiet your heart before God and meditate on one passage per day and open your heart to hear what God has to say to you. I am convinced that as you study God's Word during this time of devotion and beyond, you will taste and see that the Lord is good. The feast awaits you. Enjoy the meal!

Biblical Truth no. 1 — Acts 3:19–20 (NIV)

BE PURE BEFORE GOD

Repent then and turn to God so that your sins may be wiped out, that times of refreshing may come from the Lord (Acts 3:19-20). With a sincere heart, ask God to create in you a pure heart and renew the right spirit within you (Psalm 51:10).

As you meditate on Acts 3:19-20 and Psalm 51:10, ponder the connection between repentance, a pure heart and times of refreshing. Also, dedicate time and attention to providing an answer to the ensuing question: Why is it important to have a pure heart and renewed spirit before God? The answer is found in Matthew 5:8 and Romans 12:2.

_____

_____

_____

_____

_____

_____

_____

_____

_____

_____

_____

_____

_____

_____

Biblical Truth no. 2 — Luke 10:41–42 (NIV)

BE PRESENT WITH GOD

"Martha, Martha," the Lord answered, "you are worried and upset about many things, but few things are needed—or indeed only one. Mary has chosen what is better, and it will not be taken away from her." Just as Mary discovered what was most needful, it is also needful for you to quiet your heart before God daily and focus on Him alone.

Each day, meditate on His love for you. Acknowledge Him for His goodness, kindness and grace. Block out any thoughts that remind you of daily tasks that await you. Simply be in the moment with God and focus solely on Him.

_____

_____

_____

_____

_____

_____

_____

_____

_____

_____

_____

_____

_____

_____

Biblical Truth no. 3 — Psalm 23:1–3 (NIV)

BE CONFIDENT IN GOD

The Lord is my shepherd, I lack nothing. He makes me lie down in green pastures. He leads me beside quiet waters. He refreshes my soul. He guides me along the right paths for His name's sake.

Be convinced that God is well able to take care of everything that concerns you. There is nothing too hard for Him. He can do anything but fail. Therefore, have faith in God with all your heart and lean not to you your own understanding. In all your ways acknowledge Him and He will direct your path (Proverbs 3:5-6).

_____

_____

_____

_____

_____

_____

_____

_____

_____

_____

_____

_____

_____

_____

_____

_____

_____

BE MINDFUL OF GOD'S PROMISES

I will refresh the weary and satisfy the faint.

Trust as you spend personal time with God, He will refresh you and satisfy your soul. Trust also that the promises of God are "Yes" and "Amen." Carve out time today to search the Scriptures to increase your knowledge of the promises of God. The promises of God are yours for the asking. Studying Scripture increases our knowledge of God's will, promises and attributes. Remember, oftentimes, we have not because we ask not, and in many regards, have not received the fullness of God's promises because we are not fully aware of the promises He avows to us.

Equally, whatever we ask of God, we must ask according to His will. When we ask according to God's will, He will answer us and provide everything we need (2 Corinthians 1:20, Matthew 7:7, James 4:3).

_____

_____

_____

_____

_____

_____

_____

_____

_____

_____

_____

_____

Biblical Truth no. 5 — Proverbs 3:7–8 (NIV)

BE COMMITTED TO GOD'S PRINCIPLES AND PRECEPTS

Be not wise in your own eyes; fear the Lord and shun evil. This will bring health to your body and nourishment to your bones.

God's right way of living is the only way of living in a righteous woman's life as He knows what is best for her. Committing to the principles and precepts of God is not an option. A lifestyle contrary of God's principles and precepts results in consequences (Romans 6:23).

"For the grace of God has appeared that offers salvation to all people. It teaches us to say "No" to ungodliness and worldly passions, and to live self-controlled, upright and godly lives in this present age..." (Titus 2:11-12, NIV).

_____

_____

_____

_____

_____

_____

_____

_____

_____

_____

_____

_____

_____

_____

_____

_____

BE A REFRESHER OF SOULS FOR GOD

A generous person will prosper; whoever refreshes others will be refreshed. As you give generously to others, the same will be measured back to you. I gently encourage you to be intentional about refreshing everyone in your sphere of influence with kindness, an endearing smile, a warm embrace, a helping hand, and an encouraging word. Before you realize it, the same will be poured into your life (Luke 6:38).

_____
_____
_____
_____
_____
_____
_____
_____
_____
_____
_____
_____
_____
_____
_____
_____
_____
_____
_____

Biblical Truth no. 7 — Proverbs 3:1–6 (NIV)

Be Steadfast in Love and Faithfulness

My son, do not forget my teaching but keep my commands in your heart, for they will prolong your life many years and bring you peace and prosperity. Let love and faithfulness never leave you; bind them around your neck, write them on the tablet of your heart. Then you will win favor and a good name in the sight of God and man. Trust in the Lord with all your heart and lean not on your own understanding; in all your ways, submit to Him, and He will make your paths straight.

The journey of life is not given to the one who appears to be mighty in strength. Nor is it given to the one who appears to be progressing in life at the speed of life. The race is given to the one who endures until the end. Endurance is found in steadfast love, faithfulness to God, and God's right way of living. Bind these truths around your neck and you will endure until the end.

_____

_____

_____

_____

_____

_____

_____

_____

_____

_____

_____

_____

MORNING MANNA BITES

Give us this day our daily bread.
— Matthew 6:11, New King James Version (NKJV)

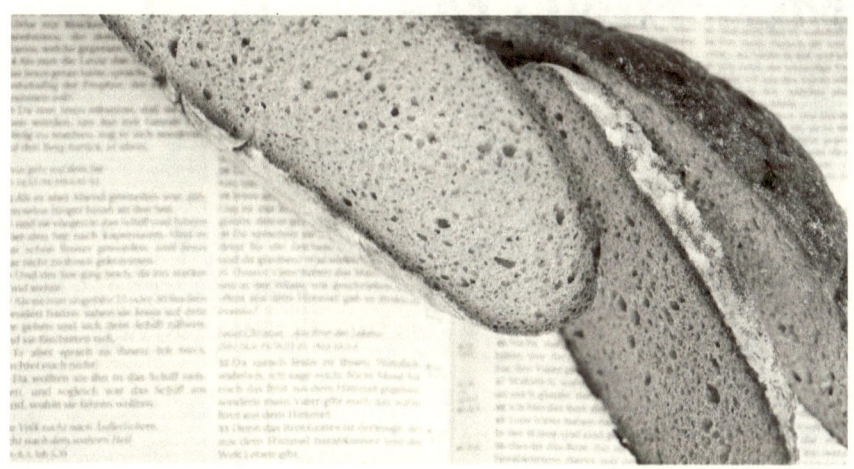

Biblical Truth no. 8 — James 1:6 (MSG)

ASK BOLDLY

Ask boldly, believing without a second thought. People who "worry [over] their prayers" are like wind-whipped waves.

— JAMES 1:6 (MSG)

I heard a powerful statement several years ago that changed my life significantly. This statement was imparted into my spirit by a woman of faith who stated, by way of a voice message she recorded on her answering machine, "Prayer is the key to the kingdom, and faith unlocks the door." Her proclamation is such a powerful statement because prayer gives believers direct access to commune with God, and faith in God paves the way for believers to receive from Him. Therefore, when you pray, pray without second-guessing whether your petitions will be granted.

In 1 John 5:14–15 (NIV), it states, "This is the confidence we have in approaching God: that if we ask anything according to His will, He hears us. And if we know that He hears us—whatever we ask—we know that we have what we asked of Him."

Therefore, be confident in knowing that when you approach the Father's throne of grace through prayer, whatever you ask according to God's will, it will come to pass. But remember to ask boldly, unswervingly, and without worry.

MORNING MANNA BITE:

Take solace in knowing that you can lay your request at God's feet, and He will answer you. When you pray, ask boldly, without doubting, believing that whatever you ask according to God's will, He will give it to you.

Ask Boldly

_____

_____

_____

_____

_____

_____

_____

_____

_____

_____

_____

_____

_____

_____

_____

_____

_____

_____

_____

_____

_____

_____

_____

_____

_____

Biblical Truth no. 9 — Matthew 6:25-30 (NIV)

Therefore, I tell you, do not worry about your life, what you will eat or drink; or about your body, what you will wear. Is not life more than food and the body more than clothes? Look at the birds of the air; they do not sow or reap or store away in barns, and yet your Heavenly Father feeds them. Are you not much more valuable than they? Can any one of you by worrying add a single hour to your life?

— MATTHEW 6:25–30 (NIV)

Several years ago, my family and I were facing a season of financial difficulty. Our cupboards were nearing empty, and the bills were more than our monetary resources could bear. But instead of worrying, I sought the Lord in prayer. I reminded God of what the writer had penned in Psalm 37:25— "I was young, and now I am old, yet I have never seen the righteous forsaken or their children begging bread" (NIV).

I recounted the life of my mother and said to God, "My mother was righteous, and your Word says I have never seen the righteous forsaken or their children begging bread." This prayer changed my life significantly because God moved expeditiously in my life, in a tangible way, and provided everything my family and I needed financially to sustain us during this season in our lives.

Worrying is the enemy of faith, and it weighs down the hearts of men and women who fall prey to its oppressive tactics (Proverbs 12:25). God does not want us to worry about anything; instead, He invites us to pray and make our requests known to Him (Philippians 4:6).

If God in His infinite power would care for the birds of the air and the lilies of the field, how much more would God do for you? Therefore, beloved, cast all your cares on God, for He cares for you (1 Peter 5:7).

Morning Manna Bite:

I am a living witness that prayer changes things. When the righteous cast their cares on God, He sustains them and will never allow them to be moved (Psalm 55:22).

So instead of worrying, *pray* and remind God of His promises. Instead of complaining, *pray* and *remind* God of His greatness. When life seems to be too much to bear, stand in faith, allowing faith to take control of your thoughts. And instead of doubting God, *believe* that when you pray according to His will, He hears you and will answer you.

Pray and Remind

_____
_____
_____
_____
_____
_____
_____
_____
_____
_____
_____
_____
_____
_____
_____
_____
_____
_____
_____
_____
_____
_____
_____
_____
_____
_____
_____
_____

A FORTIFIED FAITH

A fortified faith is the kind of faith that has been strengthened and made better against attacks. It is a faith that cannot be shaken in difficult times. This kind of faith requires one to have an active relationship with God and total belief in His mighty power. Remember, faith is the substance of things hoped for and the evidence of things not seen (Hebrews 11:1). Equally, a steadfast, continual relationship with God produces a fortified faith.

King David had a relationship with God. He sought the Lord regularly and worshipped God on a consistent basis. Prayer and praise fortified King David's faith. He was one of the most victorious kings in Bible history. Why? Because King David had a personal relationship with God. King David tapped into his source of strength by constantly communing with God. The same must ring true in our lives today for our faith to be fortified. The more personal time we spend with God, the more likely we will become more like Him (Romans 8:29). When we commune with God regularly, we learn of His great power, which in turn strengthens our faith.

MORNING MANNA BITE:

Make it a daily practice to spend time with God. Seek Him daily, and your faith will be fortified, and you will reign victorious. When Christ needed His faith to be fortified to reign triumphant at Calvary, He sought God for strength. Christ prayed earnestly before He was crucified (Matthew 26:39–44). As a result, His faith was fortified, and not only did He endure the crucifixion, but also, He triumphed victoriously (Mark 16:5–7).

A Fortified Faith

_____
_____
_____
_____
_____
_____
_____
_____
_____
_____
_____
_____
_____
_____
_____
_____
_____
_____
_____
_____
_____
_____
_____
_____
_____
_____

Speak Life

> *The tongue has the power of life and death,*
> *and those who love it will eat its fruit.*
>
> — Proverbs 18:21 (NIV)

The words we speak are powerful. What we say has the propensity to encourage or discourage, build up or tear down, or produce life or death. The world as we know it today came to be as a result of God's spoken words. In the beginning, God said, "Let there be," and every subsequent word He spoke came to fruition (Genesis 1). But note in the Book of Genesis, the words God spoke were positive. Instead of grumbling and complaining, God chose to speak words that produced positive outcomes. He chose to speak words that illuminated light and life into Earth's formless, dark and void state-of-being.

As daughters of the Most High, we have been granted the same speaking authority. According to Job 22:28 (KJV), "Thou shalt also decree a thing, and it shall be established unto thee: and the light shall shine upon thy ways." God has granted us the power to decree life into dead situations. In addition, the very words we speak can move mountains in our lives. However, there is a caveat to these truths; the words we speak must align with the Word of God and mixed with faith to produce positive life-changing results (Matthew 21:21).

Morning Manna Bite:

The Word of God is absolute and infallible. It contains everything we need to overcome any situation. It is a divine instrument designed by God to help us fulfill our God-ordained purposes and live a victorious life. Having said that, I encourage you to fill your mouth with words that produce life and not death. Speak the Word of God. Speak what God is saying, not what you see or feel. Grumbling and complaining produce negative outcomes. But positive confessions; words that align with the Word of God, produce life.

Equally, I encourage you to fill your heart with the Word of God because the words you speak are directly connected to what dwells in your heart. Christ said, "The mouth speaks what the heart is full of" (Matthew 12:34, NIV). A cantankerous heart produces cantankerous words. A disparaging heart produces disparaging words. A holier-than-thou heart produces judgmental words. An ungrateful heart produces bitter words. An angry heart produces hurtful words. A bitter heart produces sardonic words.

A heart filled with the Word of God, however, produces life. Words that are loving, kind, gentle, edifying, uplifting, graceful, filled with faith, and peaceful spring forth out of a heart that is filled with the Word of God, produce life.

Speak Life

_____
_____
_____
_____
_____
_____
_____
_____
_____
_____
_____
_____
_____
_____
_____
_____
_____
_____
_____
_____
_____
_____
_____
_____
_____
_____
_____

Biblical Truth no. 12 — Colossians 3:2 (NLT)

EXAMINATION: DETERMINE WHAT MATTERS MOST

Think about the things of heaven, not the things of earth.
— COLOSSIANS 3:2 (NLT)

Does it really matter if the people you value most rally around you to offer support or a lend a helping hand whenever you need it? Does it really matter if your colleagues favor you or not? Does it really matter if the Boaz you thought would be your knight in shining armor marries someone else? Does it really matter if your relationship with your biological parents is broken and dysfunctional? Or does it really matter if the recent divorce you experienced was a bitter ending because the person you fell head over hills for cheated on you or left you for someone else?

What really matters most in the life of a God-fearing woman? I am glad you asked. The final analysis is what matters most for all humankind. On the day of judgment, each of us will appear before the judgment seat of Christ to receive what is due to us (2 Corinthians 5:10). When we stand before God, the final analysis will not be contingent upon how others treated us. The final analysis will be determined by the life we lived.

MORNING MANNA BITE:

In the final analysis, hearing God say, "Well done, my good and faithful servant," is what will matter most. I gently remind you to set your mind on heavenly things. Aim to please God and not people. Aim to live your life by God's standards and not the opinions or approval of others. Aim to let your light shine before others, that they may see your good deeds and glorify your Father in heaven. And aim to love every single person in your present life, your past life, and your circle of influence because we are nothing without love (1 Corinthians 13:2).

Of greater truth, anyone who says she loves God and hates her brother or sister is a liar. Anyone that does not love her brother or sister, whom she has seen, cannot love God, whom she hath not seen (1 John 4:20). In the final analysis, what will our heavenly Father say to you?

Examination: Determine What Matters Most

Biblical Truth no. 13 — Ephesians 6:10-13 (NIV)

ARSENAL PREPARATION: THE WEAPONS OF OUR WARFARE ARE NOT CARNAL

Finally, be strong in the Lord and in His mighty power. Put on the full armor of God so that you can take your stand against the devil's schemes. For our struggle is not against flesh and blood but against the rulers, against the authorities, against the powers of this dark world, and against the spiritual forces of evil in the heavenly realms.

— EPHESIANS 6:10–13 (NIV)

Have you ever felt like you were in battle with your spouse, children, family members, coworkers, or communal neighbors? Here recently, have you been in conflict with someone close to you who, for some odd reason, makes you feel as if every waking moment is a never-ending battle? Truthfully, whatever conflict you are experiencing that gives off the illusion that you are in battle with a person or persons is a tactic of the adversary to mislead and distract you. The battle before you is not against flesh and blood but against rulers, authorities, powers of darkness of this world, and spiritual forces of evil in the heavenly realm (Ephesians 6:10–13). The very moment a believer grasps this truth and prepares daily for spiritual battle, the fashion in which he or she responds to hard-pressed situations or challenges of life will change immensely.

Daily preparation for spiritual battle and ultimately victory over the adversary are achieved by standing on the Word of God and entering battle with the right arsenal: the belt of truth buckled around your waist; the breastplate of righteousness in place; your feet fitted with the readiness that comes from the gospel of peace; the shield of faith; the helmet of salvation; and the sword of the Spirit (Ephesians 6:14–7). Clothe yourself daily with these spiritual weapons, and you will outwit the enemy's schemes.

MORNING MANNA BITE:

Always remember that the battle confronting you is never a person; it is rulers, authorities, powers of this dark world, and spiritual forces of evil in the heavenly realms. Put on the full armor of God daily, and you will stand victorious against any tactic the enemy is attempting to use to discourage you. In addition, meditate on 2 Corinthians 10:4–7 often. This passage is a kind reminder of the divine power women of God possess.

Arsenal Preparation

_____
_____
_____
_____
_____
_____
_____
_____
_____
_____
_____
_____
_____
_____
_____
_____
_____
_____
_____
_____
_____
_____
_____
_____
_____
_____

Biblical Truth no. 14 — Proverbs 13:22 (KJV)

LEGACY

A good man leaveth an inheritance to his children's children: and the wealth of the sinner is laid up for the just.

— PROVERBS 13:22 (KJV)

If a good man would leave an inheritance significant enough to reach his children's children, how much more would our Heavenly Father leave behind for His daughters and sons? There is no need to question whether God has an inheritance for His children because He promises to give those who choose Him life, eternal life, grace, acceptance, compassion, and love. The righteous can rest assured that God's promises are yes and amen (2 Corinthians 1:20). When God makes a promise, it is backed by more than shallow words or noble intents. Therefore, every child of God can rejoice in knowing that everything God promises, He will perform because God is not a man that He should lie or change His mind about what He has promised the Just (Numbers 23:19).

Time and again, I have benefited from being a child of God. The day I accepted Christ into my heart—November 14, 1993—my life changed for the better. Twenty-five years later, I can boldly state that "God has never forsaken me, and He has *always* made a way out of despair, trouble, and disappointment whenever the odds seemed as though they were stacked against me."

MORNING MANNA BITE:

Just as God has been faithful to me, if you trust and believe in His promises and live according to His principles and precepts, He will do the same for you. God has left behind a LEGACY for His righteous daughters and sons that extends from generation to generation for thousands of years. We can hold fast to the LEGACY God has left behind for us, which is profoundly this: Life (John 10:10), Eternal life (John 3:16), Grace (2 Timothy 1:9), Acceptance (Ephesians 1:3–6), Compassion (2 Corinthians 1:3–4), and Years of lavished love (Exodus 20:6, NLT). I encourage you to meditate often on these Scriptures as they are kind reminders of the LEGACY God has left behind for His children.

Legacy

_____
_____
_____
_____
_____
_____
_____
_____
_____
_____
_____
_____
_____
_____
_____
_____
_____
_____
_____
_____
_____
_____
_____
_____
_____
_____

A COMMAND TO LOVE

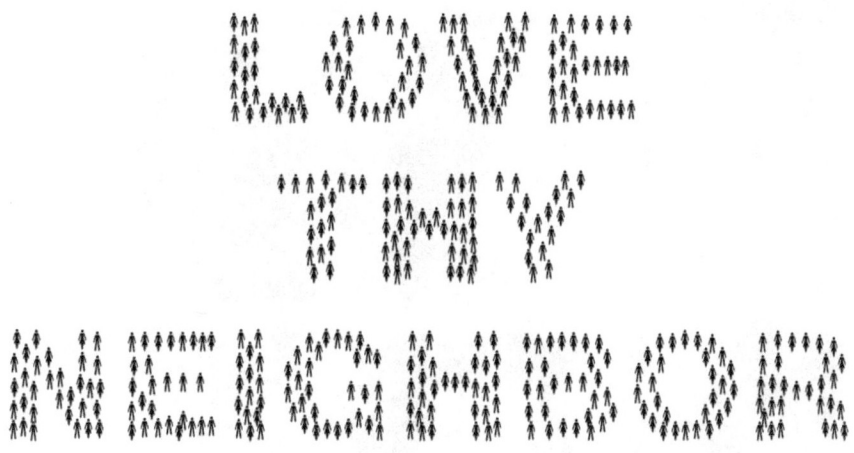

A Command to Love: A Necessary Action

Woman of worth, rejoice in the Lord always. Again, I say, "Rejoice," for you were created by God to be an extension of His love in the earth. Why would God mold you in such a way? Because the world around you is in dire need of love. And God wants to use you to deliver the difference. He wants to use you to set the captives free. Freedom begins with love because love serves as a bridge over troubled waters. It is the instrument God uses to redeem the lost, comfort troubled minds, heal the wounded, and mend broken hearts. In times like these, when love seems nonexistent, God proves otherwise.

In many regards, the very blessing or breakthrough we are standing in faith for is directly connected to our willingness to walk in the way of love. God commands us to walk in the way of love because love conquers all. In addition, God has charged us to love without boundaries because love knows no boundaries. When we walk in the way of love, our hearts are at peace. May you find consolation and peace as you meditate on the ensuing Scriptures and hold fast to God's teachings:

◊ **1 Corinthians 13**

The true essence of love.

◊ **John 15:12**

My command is this: Love each other as I have loved you.

◊ **James 13:35**

By this, everyone will know that you are my disciples if you love one another.

◊ **1 John 4:7–8**

Beloved, let us love one another, for love is from God, and whoever loves has been born of God and knows God. Anyone who does not love does not know God because God is love.

◊ **1 John 4:20**

Whoever claims to love God yet hates a brother or sister is a liar. For whoever does not love their brother and sister, whom they have seen, cannot love God, whom they have not seen.

LOVE CHARGE: WALK IN THE WAY OF LOVE

Love is greater than faith; it is greater than hope, and it conquers all. Love testifies of God because love is from God (1 Corinthians 13:13; 1 John 4:7). When we walk in the way of love, we demonstrate one of God's greatest commands. Daily, God commands us to put on love because "love binds everything together in harmony" (Colossians 3:14). Equally relevant, the greatest commandment in the law is to love the Lord your "God with all your heart and with all your soul and with all your mind. This is the great and first commandment. And a second is like it: You shall love your neighbor as yourself" (Matthew 22:36–40). Therefore, walking in the way of love is not an option for followers of Christ. Every born-again believer is called to always demonstrate and display love. To fulfill the call, however, believers must know the truth about love and demonstrate it accordingly. During ancient biblical times, through the divine instruction of God, the apostle Paul proclaimed and demonstrated God's right way of loving others. Even today, standards of love set forth by the apostle Paul remain apropos to modern-day Christians.

In 1 Corinthians 13, the apostle Paul denotes a narrative about love that reveals to the biblical audience the true essence of love. When we meditate on 1 Corinthians 13, we become keenly aware that love is more than words; it is expressed best through actions because love requires one to act. Additionally, through our personal experiences as children of God, we know that God's love is unconditional and eternal. We also know that love is more than shallow words because God has always committed to loving us even when we did not deserve His love. According to the apostle Paul, "love is patient. Love is kind. It does not envy. It does not boast. It is not proud. It does not dishonor others. It is not self-seeking. It is not easily angered. It keeps no record of wrongs. Love does not delight in evil but rejoices with the truth. It always protects, always trusts, always hopes, always perseveres. Love never fails" (1 Corinthians 13:4–8, NIV). When followers of Christ demonstrate love in this manner, they reflect who God is, embrace His standards for love, and display to others the love of God in action. In short, love is a commitment to act in a manner that proves its validity. Love conquers all, and a life void of love is bankrupt (1 Corinthians 13).

Even further, love is the vehicle God uses to abolish unforgiveness, bitterness, malice, pride, anger, impatience, and ill behaviors. Love has no contingencies. It is not contingent upon emotional hype or conditional circumstances. It is a constant decision to act in a specific manner regardless of the circumstance or issue. God's love for humanity caused Him to act, sacrificing His only begotten Son for the remission of our sins. And love caused God to respond to mankind's need for redemption through sending His only begotten son into the earth to demonstrate love in action. A primary tactic of the adversary is to distract us and lure us away from God through antilove invitations to model pseudo love fashioned after worldly standards, standards driven by emotions that stem from the lust of the flesh, selfish gain, deceitful passions, the lust of the eyes, and pride. John 2:16–17 proclaims that "For everything in the world—the lust of the flesh, the lust of the eyes, and the pride of life—comes not from the Father but from the world. The world and its desires pass away, but whoever does the will of God lives forever" (NIV). Ultimately, the adversary of love desires to keep us from walking in the way of love according to God's standards because the adversary of love understands the power of demonstrating love the way God commands.

In 2017, a time when I endured multiple attacks that buffeted intensely at my capacity to love, God summoned me to love more. I truly had no other recourse but to lean and depend on God because I could not love according to His standards in my own strength. God is amazing and faithful because He guided me though every test of my love and empowered me to overcome with victory. Today I am liberated and victorious because God carried me, taught me, and empowered me to love in spite of what I was going through. During this very challenging time in my life, God also instructed me to invite my husband, Paul, daughters, Aubrianna and Kiyah, and ten covenant sisters in Christ to join me in a twenty-one-day love fast. The following year, God called me to invite my sisters, closest spiritual sisters, and women residing in the Central Florida region to join me in the Twenty-One Days of Love for Her Mission and Scatter Love Campaign. The book you are holding in your hands is the result of revelations and truths God revealed to me as I acquiesced to His instructions, for two consecutive years, to love *more*. To date, God continues to commission me to love *more*.

I have come to realize that love is the answer to everything we experience in life. Love conquers all. And love causes the enemy to tremble because it combats the adversary's deceitful attempts to draw us away from God and one another. In contrast, the enemy does not flee from believers who are rude, impatient, thoughtless, or unforgiving. He fears nothing from loveless sermons, loveless actions, loveless words, and loveless relationships. In fact, the adversary of love mocks our religion, snickers at our performance-based efforts, but agonizes when we love as God commands. When we demonstrate and display love by way of forgiveness, patience, kindness, long suffering, consideration, and humility, God is glorified, we are victorious, and those around us are given permission to model the same. As we strive earnestly to walk in the way of love and hold fast to God's teachings found in Holy Scripture, let us be mindful of His right way of demonstrating love. As you remain steadfast and committed to walking in the way of love, may an overabundance of love be reciprocated back to you one hundredfold.

A Command to Love

_____

_____

_____

_____

_____

_____

_____

_____

_____

_____

_____

_____

_____

_____

_____

_____

_____

_____

_____

_____

_____

_____

_____

_____

_____

_____

HERSTORY: DAILY DEVOTIONAL LETTERS TO INSPIRE HER HEART

Biblical Truth no. 15 — Jeremiah 29:11 (NIV)

HIS DESTINED DIAMOND: ALL THINGS ARE WORKING TOGETHER FOR YOUR GOOD

"For I know the plans I have for you," declares the Lord, "plans to prosper you and not to harm you, plans to give you hope and a future."

— JEREMIAH 29:11 (NIV)

Beloved Sister,

Hidden hundreds of miles beneath the earth's surface, a rare, beautiful find is discovered when deep volcanic eruptions carry to Earth's outward habitat one of the most precious stones in the world: a diamond. The extraordinary voyage that thrusts a diamond to Earth's view is a miracle indeed considering the level of extreme heat and pressure required to finish a diamond's final stage of development. One would assume that heat and pressure would destroy anything in its fiery fury and distressing force, but in the case of a diamond, these elements combined work together to produce a precious, prized gem.

The purpose of a diamond is settled long before its discovery. A diamond is purposed to be awe-inspiring, brilliant, and unbreakable. Destined to be revealed in all its splendor, a diamond emerges through the darkest and harshest of conditions. Despite adverse elements surrounding a diamond in its infancy, every aspect of a diamond's development process ultimately works together for its greatness and spectacular discovery.

The largest diamond ever discovered was called the Cullinan Diamond and weighed in at an amazing 3,106 carats or 1.33 pounds. This stunning diamond was discovered in 1905 in South Africa. The owner of the mine and South African leaders gifted the diamond to King Edward. This diamond was so brilliant, it was fit for a king (Brilliant Earth Blog, 2018). Indisputably, diamonds are incomparable to any other gem. Diamonds are destined to radiate awe-inspiring beauty. I announce to you that you too are a destined diamond, a gem fit for the King of Kings. You were purposed by God to radiate the splendor of His glory, brilliance, and power throughout the earth. Although the fiery trials and pressures of life currently confronting you may seem to be working against you, I urge you to stand firm in your faith, remain steadfast in the Lord, and not to lean to your own understanding because in the life of a righteous woman, all things work together for her good (Romans 8:28). When God finishes His masterful work in you during this season in your life, you will emerge from beneath the very thing that seems to be more than you can bear, radiating the splendor and glory of God as the precious prized gem He predestined you to be.

The fact that you are reading this commentary is not by happenstance. This devotional was predestined to be in your reach because God wants to gently remind you that He is purifying and refining you. Just as a diamond endures great pressure and heat to reach its full potential, the fiery trials and pressures of life God's women of righteousness endure work together to help them fulfill their God-given purposes. I gently remind you that when life's challenges seem more than you can bear, remember, God is refining and pruning you for greater victories. Be confident in knowing that the fiery trials and pressures of life confronting you today will not destroy you if you embrace God's right way of doing things, remain steadfast in your faith, and permit yourself to be polished by Him.

Oftentimes, when we are confronted with trials and tribulations, our longing to be delivered out of our troubles is greater than our desire to wait patiently for God to use the pressures of life to finish His work within us. Of a truth, we mature fully during times of great pressure when we acquiesce to God's pruning and refining processes. "You know that under pressure, your faith life is forced into the open and shows its true colors. So do not try to get out of anything prematurely. Let it do its work so you become mature and well-developed, not deficient in any way" (James 1:3–4). Your life experiences in days of old as well as your current circumstances are orchestrated by God to work together for your good. Now I must say, there is a caveat to this truth. All that happens to us works together for our good when we love God with all our hearts, live according to His principles and precepts, and pursue the plans He has for us (Romans 8:28, James 1:22–25). When our lifestyles are evident of these things, the precious diamond God predestined us to be will miraculously shine forth with unbreakable strength and power.

Throughout the Bible, God clearly demonstrates our worth and value. There is nothing on this earth that God values more than womankind and mankind. Just as a diamond is incomparable to any other gem, so are we incomparable to anything on this earth in the eyes of God. Rest assured, *all* things are working together for the righteous woman's good because God's making a diamond out of her. Even greater, Isaiah 43:2–4 declares, "When you pass through the waters, I will be with you; and when you pass through the rivers, they will not sweep over you. When you walk through the fire, you will not be burned; the flames will not set you ablaze. For I am the Lord your God, the Holy One of Israel, your Savior; I give Egypt for your ransom, Cush and Seba in your stead. Since you are precious and honored in my sight, and because I love you, I will give people in exchange for you, nations in exchange for your life." (NIV). Despite the pressures of life and fiery trials you have experienced or are currently walking through, trust that everything associated with this time in your life is working together for your good. In due season, this process of pressure and fire will add another facet of spiritual growth, strength, and beauty to your life. Equally, "you shall be a crown of beauty in the hand of the Lord and a royal diadem in the hand of God" (Isaiah 63:2, ESV).

Therefore, be encouraged in the Lord and remember, the fiery trials and pressures of life confronting you today are strategically designed to refine and prepare you for your God-given purpose. Of a truth, your purpose was settled long before you were born. God's plans for you are good and not evil. He has an expected end for you (Jeremiah 29:11), and God is always fighting for you. "For the Lord your God is He who goes with you to fight for you against your enemies, to give you the victory" (Deuteronomy 20:4). Even greater, "in all this, you greatly rejoice, though now for a little while you may have had to suffer grief in all kinds of trials. These have come so that the proven genuineness of your faith— of greater worth than gold, which perishes even though refined by fire— may result in praise, glory, and honor when the Messiah is revealed" (1 Peter 1:6–7). Therefore, take solace in knowing that it does not matter how intense the pressures of life and fiery trials confronting you today may be; if you trust in God with all your heart and live according to His commands, He will not allow the cares of life to overshadow His plans for you because diamonds are made under pressure, and you, my dearest sister in the Lord, are His destined diamond.

DAILY DEVOTIONAL SCRIPTURES:

◊ Meditate on Jeremiah 29:11, James 1:3–4, Romans 8:28, Isaiah 43:2–4, Isaiah 63:2, and Deuteronomy 20:4.

LOVE CHARGE:

◊ Have faith. Encourage another sister to do the same. Allow perseverance to finish its work. God is making a diamond out of you.

My Sister's Keeper,

Felicia D. Shelton, His Destined Diamond

His Destined Diamond: All Things Are Working Together for Your Good

_____
_____
_____
_____
_____
_____
_____
_____
_____
_____
_____
_____
_____
_____
_____
_____
_____
_____
_____
_____
_____
_____
_____
_____
_____

Biblical Truth no. 16 — 1 Corinthians 13:1 (MSG)

WHAT'S LOVE GOT TO DO WITH IT? EVERYTHING!

If I speak with human eloquence and angelic ecstasy but don't love, I'm nothing but the creaking of a rusty gate.

— 1 CORINTHIANS 13:1 (MSG)

Greetings, Beloved Sister in Christ!

In the mid-eighties, Tina Turner, an iconic American pop star, released a famous love ballet titled "What's Love Got to Do with It?" This popular ballet is an antilove song that suggests love is a secondhand emotion that leads to a broken heart. For decades—and I dare say to date—women and men alike, from all walks of life, revel over this song because they enjoy the rhythm of the song and, in many regards, agree with Turner's argument against love. Although Turner's antilove song excelled on pop charts nationwide in its heyday, the characteristic of love portrayed in this ballet is contrary to God's definition of love. In contrast, the Word of God, as noted in 1 Corinthians 13, speaks of love from a different perspective, revealing the true essence of love. In this sacred Scripture, a positive narrative about love comes to light. In fact, according to 1 Corinthians 13, wherever there is an existence of love, patience, kindness, selflessness, compassion, humility, and protection from harm are sure to abound.

Conversely, contrary to Turner's argument against love, a multitude of positive attributes are noted in the Word of God as it relates to love. As a born-again believer, to defend the characteristics of love, one must fully understand and agree that the truth about love is based on God's definition, not Turner's definition, not the world's definition, and not mankind or womankind's definition. The world's definition of love, in more cases than not, is based on emotions, driven by the lust of the eye, and motivated by selfish gain. Men and women's definitions of love are oftentimes based on their personal experiences, teachings about love from influential people in their lives, or what they were sublimely exposed to through love ballets, love-related sitcoms, or the media. Many of these outlets portray love as a physical attraction that inevitably leads to sexual rendezvous and short-lived relationships. However, when love is viewed through these lenses, it is misconstrued. But today please allow me to gently debunk these fallacies about love because love is far greater than a secondhand emotion that leads to a broken heart.

To begin, I believe the birthing of "What's Love Got to Do with It?" was a strategic ploy by the adversary of love to deceive believers and nonbelievers into avoiding loving others because the enemy knows how relevant love is when conveyed as God commands. Moreover, there are a plethora of benefits associated with loving one another. As a result, it bears repeating that love is not a secondhand emotion that leads to a broken heart. In fact, love always protects, always trusts, always hopes, and always perseveres (1 Corinthians 13:7). In addition, the Word of God makes it clear that all the worldly intellectual knowledge, all the supernatural understanding in the world, and all the faith in the world will benefit us nothing if we do not possess love. Consequently, a life void of God's love is lonely, empty, and meaningless. Love is the reason God created us; therefore, if we do not learn to give and receive love as God intends, our lives will amount to nothing (1 Corinthians 14). When we love as the Word of God commands, we reflect the true nature of God as well as our belief in what God says. Even further, love knows no boundaries. Love is not restricted by race, social class, sexual orientation, or religious association. Love in the life of a believer transcends social constructs. God commands us to love not just our family, friends, or individuals we deem worthy of our love but even our enemies.

With regard to the question Turner posed in her antilove ballet, my response is absolutely, unequivocally "everything" because the Word of God clearly states that love is what identifies our discipleship to the world. "Your love for one another will prove to the world that you are my disciples" (John 13:35, New Living Translation). Further, God loves us so much that

He sent Christ as a sacrificial Lamb to die for the remission of our sins so that we would know the full measure of God's love. Equally, love refused to abandon the call of the cross so that we would know the width and length and depth and height of Christ's love for us (Ephesians 3:18). It was love that compelled Christ to endure the crucifixion to ensure our salvation. And thus, it was love that caused Christ to forgive His accusers. Therefore, the next time someone implies that love is a secondhand emotion that leads to a broken heart, remind them of the Lord of the Cross, our Risen King, Yeshua Hamashiach. Remind them that love compelled our Lord and Savior to render his broken body for womankind and mankind so that we too would experience the true essence of love.

If for some reason your heart has been broken, wounded, or bruised countless times in the name of love, I am a living witness that God's loving hands are well able to gather all the scattered pieces of your heart and mend it back together again. God can heal you everywhere you have been broken. Perhaps you have a bad taste in your spirit about love. I encourage you to open your heart to receive the love of God and give love another chance. Whatever you do, do not give up on loving others or receiving love. The enemy of love that gives love a bad name is pseudo love disguised in men and women who attempt to love others without first loving God. Unfortunately, when we open our hearts to receive love from individuals who have not surrendered their lives totally to God, we do not experience love as God intends. Ultimately, any attempt to love others without having a personal relationship with God results in pseudo love. To fully love others, one must first love God. The lack thereof leads to broken relationships, broken hearts, and broken dreams. This truth is the totality of what leads to broken hearts, not love itself. A bit of advice I highly recommend that has proven to work in my life is the following formula, which is guaranteed to produce real love: righteousness (living in harmony with God) + patience, kindness, long suffering, forgiveness, and humility = love as God intends. When our lifestyles reflect these actions, we will experience the kind of love that has everything to do with the relevance, influence, and power of love.

Daily Devotional Scriptures:

◊ Meditate on 1 Corinthians 13, John 13:35, Ephesians 3:17–19, Matthew 22:37, Luke 6:32–36, 1 John 3:1, John 14:15, 1 Peter 4:8, and Proverbs 17:9.

Love Charge:

◊ Strive daily to walk in love, aiming to model the attributes of love (patience, kindness, forgiveness, humility). Be patient with the process. Remember, each of us is a work in progress, and God is faithful to finish the work He has begun in us.

◊ Forgive everyone who has hurt you.

My Sister's Keeper,

Felicia D. Shelton, His Destined Diamond

What's Love Got to Do with It? Everything!

_____
_____
_____
_____
_____
_____
_____
_____
_____
_____
_____
_____
_____
_____
_____
_____
_____
_____
_____
_____
_____
_____
_____
_____
_____

Biblical Truth no. 17 — Galatians 5:22-23 (NIV)

WHEN LIFE GIVES YOU LEMONS, CHOOSE TO WALK IN THE FRUIT OF THE SPIRIT

But the fruit of the Spirit is love, joy, peace, forbearance, kindness, goodness, faithfulness, gentleness, and self-control.
— GALATIANS 5:22–23 (NIV)

Greetings, Woman of Worth!

Several years ago, someone very close to me did the unthinkable thing: she betrayed me. The aftermath of this incident left me wounded, broken, and disappointed. To add insult to injury, others around me knew of the incident long before I did, including someone who was closer to me than the person who had betrayed me, but she later admitted that she had chosen to withhold the matter from me because she did not want to hurt me. However, it was only a matter of time when the truth would be revealed. Inevitably, I learned of the matter. Truthfully, it does not matter how long an act of deceit or betrayal is hidden; eventually, it will come to light, right? As my wise mother taught me, what is done in the dark will come to light. Moreover, "there is nothing hidden that will not be disclosed and nothing concealed that will not be known or brought out into the open" (Luke 8:13, NIV). Thankfully, someone I had least expected cared enough about me to inform me that the person I thought was my dear friend had betrayed me. This was an offense that angered me immediately when I had learned of what had been done against me, but Holy Spirit reminded me not to sin by letting anger control me (Ephesians 4:26, NLT). Albeit controlling my anger was not an easy feat, I did not allow it to control my thoughts or actions.

It is one thing for someone close to you to betray you, and no one else is privy of the matter but you and the perpetrator; however, it is another thing to be clueless that someone in your inner circle has betrayed you, and others close to you are aware of the incident but choose to withhold the information from you. Not surprisingly, isn't this kind of cunning behavior the very nature of the adversary of our faith? Isn't it just like the nature of the enemy of our faith to feed off deceit and deception, to wound, discourage, and defeat us? In addition, whenever the enemy plots to wound us severely, he targets someone close to us, generally an individual who pretends to be in our corner when, in all actuality, they are not. The adversary is fully aware that we least expect our family, friends, or close acquaintances to harm us. So, the enemy waits patiently for a willing vessel in our inner circle to lure away from God and us to join allies with him to launch a devastating attack against us. The incident I am referring to was certainly a time in my life that the enemy hit me below the belt and wounded me deeply because I trusted the individual who had betrayed me and loved her like a sister. Not only was she a close friend of mine, but also, she was a close friend of my family. The pain I had endured as a consequence of this incident was one of the most distressing times in my life. The most hurtful aspect of the matter was the deceptive role this individual played and her lack of consideration of how her actions would impact our friendship, families, and ultimately our lives. Her choice to betray me left me no other recourse but to believe that the sisterly bond I thought we had forged over the years was meaningless to her. This reality was the most painful truth I had to come to grips with.

Without question, this was a very sour time in my life. But instead of allowing the sourness of deception, betrayal, pain, unforgiveness, bitterness, or resentment to set up residence in my heart, I chose to walk in the fruit of the Spirit. Was walking in the fruit of the Spirit during this very challenging time in my life easy? Absolutely not. But Father Yah, my great Deliverer and the Defender behind me, gave me the tools I needed to overcome this testing time as the victor and not the victim. He used this incident to make me sweeter and not sour. God taught me the importance of forgiveness, the power of love, and how to love through painful situations without constraints. Given the small community I had lived in at the time, it was quite clear to me that the vast majority of my friends, family, and associates knew of the matter. However, God spoke to me loud and clear and said to me, "You are going to show everyone around you how to love as I have taught you." And so I did.

I chose to forgive the individual who had betrayed me and made a decision to love her anyway. I chose to respond based on the Word of God and not my emotions. Every time I encountered her, regardless of the locality, I greeted her with a friendly hug, exchanged kind words with her, and did my best not to slam her into a wall. Oh yes, although I had forgiven her and chosen to treat her as God commanded me, my flesh wanted to give her a piece of my mind and a piece of my fist every now and then. But I knew that acting out of Godly character would not please God; neither would it glorify Him. In all honesty, my journey to victory was laden with a lot of negative emotions. Albeit these negative emotions were very real and quite challenging at times, I was intentional about not allowing these emotions to control my actions because I knew that God required so much more of me. Every decision we make in life, both good and bad, is directly connected to *choice*. Consequently, where we are currently in life is closely correlated to the choices we have made in the past. We can choose to follow God, or we can choose to follow the enemy of our faith. I have learned firsthand that the greater reward is always in following God.

Regardless of the pain and disappointment I had experienced throughout this test, I chose God's right way of doing things instead of reacting based on my emotions. I chose to look beyond the offense and faults of the person who had betrayed me. I chose love over resentment. I chose to see the greater mission at work. God's mission is that none should perish and that we would be instruments of His love at all times, in all situations. In all actuality, this individual was in need of forgiveness. She was also in need of God's love and deliverance. I realized that it was not my place to put her where I thought she belonged; nor was it my duty to straighten her out because she had betrayed me. God is the one who handles these types of offenses, and He does it with ease. Equally, it does not matter what others do to us; what matters most is how we respond. The more I chose to share the love of God with her, the less painful it became for me to love her unconditionally. Eventually, I was liberated from the aftermath of this very trying time in my life.

Abiding by the principles and precepts of God is not always easy; however, as women of God, it is imperative that we choose God's right way of living in all situations instead of the world's way or our own. After all, God knows what is best for us. When we respond to life's ups and downs in Christ-like manners, we reign with Christ in victory. Truthfully, ungodly characteristics—which oftentimes stem from a lifestyle of unrighteousness, unforgiveness, bitterness, and resentment—imprison the person who chooses to harbor and act upon negative emotions. Ultimately, we become slaves to sin when we choose to permit ungodly emotions to prevent us from walking in the fruit of the Spirit. Even greater, we are prisoners to sin when we fail to live by God's principles and precepts. But there is good news. Walking in the fruit of the Spirit empowers us to live a life of freedom, wholeness, joy, and peace. Each of us must give an account to God for our individual actions, not the actions of others. As women of God, we must exemplify the fruit of the Spirit when life gives us lemons.

I find it very intriguing that the very first attribute noted in the fruit of the Spirit passage of Scripture is *love*. Truthfully, everything hinges on love. Love is the greatest gift we can extend to others because God is love. Love is greater than faith. Love is greater than hope. And consequently, we are nothing without love (1 Corinthians 13). Christ made it clear to the disciples that they would be known as His disciples by the love they demonstrated to one another (John 13:35). Notice in John 13:35 that Christ did not place an emphasis on the disciples' titles, social statuses, crafty words, powerful sermons, intellects, or pedigrees as attributes that would make them known as His disciples. Instead, Christ emphasized that their love for one another would distinguish their discipleship. Still today, love is what sets apart the righteous from the unrighteous. As women of God, we are called to love one another despite our faults or shortcomings. Doing so reveals the very nature of God and conveys to the world who we really are. When our guiding mantra is founded on loving one another as God commands, coupled with a conscious effort to walk in the fruit of the Spirit daily, there is no device, tactic, or scheme the enemy can use to prevent us from reigning victorious in Christ.

In every hardship, test, or trial, we must realize that God intends for everything we experience in life to work together for our good. But the enemy of our faith desires to use our tests and tribulations to sift us as wheat. The enemy of our faith longs to steal our joy, peace, happiness, sisterly relationships, and, most importantly, love. If he can steal these things from us, he has the propensity to destroy us. Nonetheless, the enemy of our faith can only destroy us if we give him permission to do so by choosing his way instead of God's way. The enemy's devices are not fair, and he most certainly does not play by the rules because his ultimate goal is to separate us from God. Whenever we harbor bitterness, unforgiveness, resentment, and deceit and live a lifestyle of sin, we give the enemy permission to wreak havoc in our lives. A consistent lifestyle of sin brings with it serious consequences, consequences that result in separation from God. "Behold, the Lord's hand is not shortened that it cannot save or His ear dull that it cannot hear; but your iniquities have made a separation between you and your God, and your sins have hidden His face from you so that He does not hear" (Isaiah 59:1–2).

As previously mentioned, sin separates us from God; therefore, if the enemy can deceive us into believing that a lifestyle of consistent sin does not have serious consequences, he has a greater propensity to achieve his ultimate goal. Likewise, once we are separated from God, the enemy gains momentum in defeating us because separation from God leads to spiritual weakness and ultimately spiritual death. As women of God, let us strive to live a lifestyle of righteousness. Let us strive to walk in the fruit of the Spirit when life gives us lemons. Throughout your life course, at some time or another, you will find yourself in bitter, painful situations, but remember, when life gives you lemons, choose to walk in the fruit of the Spirit. When we walk in the Spirit, we will not fulfill the lust of the flesh (Galatians 5:16). "Anything less than God's holy standard is sin" (Pastor William McDowell, Deeper Fellowship Church, Orlando, Florida).

DAILY DEVOTIONAL SCRIPTURES:

◊ Meditate on Galatians 5:22–23, 1 Corinthians 13, and Galatians 5:16.

LOVE CHARGE:

◊ Choose to demonstrate love, joy, peace, forbearance, kindness, goodness, faithfulness, gentleness, and self-control. Display these attributes daily.
◊ Walk in the Spirit, and you will not fulfill the lust of the flesh (Galatians 5:16).

Lovingly,

Felicia D. Shelton, His Destined Diamond

When Life Gives You Lemons, Choose to Walk in the Fruit of the Spirit

_____

_____

_____

_____

_____

_____

_____

_____

_____

_____

_____

_____

_____

_____

_____

_____

_____

_____

_____

_____

_____

_____

_____

_____

_____

THE Q-TIP CHALLENGE: GOD WILL PROVIDE THE SLING AND STONE

So David triumphed over the Philistine with a sling and stone; without a sword in his hand, he struck down the Philistine and killed him.

— 1 SAMUEL 17:50 (NIV)

Greetings, God's Prized Creation!

While pursuing my undergraduate degree, one of my professors introduced me to a very powerful, life-changing concept, the Q-TIP philosophy. The acronym Q-TIP stands for the following: quit taking it personally. To this day, this philosophy is one of my guiding mantras. Time and again, this concept has helped me maintain a positive disposition in challenging times. This approach has also changed the way I conduct myself in the vast majority of situations. In more cases than not, whenever we take things personally, our vision is skewed because we are so focused on the self that we cannot see the bigger picture. Interestingly though, the professor who had introduced this viewpoint to me was one of the most challenging professors I encountered in college. Her attitude toward me was very rash, rude, and outright disrespectful. She was a giant in her own right as a consequence of her position of authority and power. And trust me, her demeanor made it clear that she was fully aware of her social status. Nonetheless, one of my spiritual sisters and I were enrolled in the class together. Having her alongside me to share this phase of my educational journey made the experience a whole lot sweeter. In an effort to conquer Professor Goliath, my spiritual sister and I worked together to complete our final group project. Ultimately, the goal of our strategic efforts was to complete the course with a A+. Consequently, I finished the class with an A-. After discovering how I had fared in the class, I thought to myself, *What a slap in the face!* At the beginning of this debacle, it was hard for me to Q-TIP because I knew from the depth of my heart that I did not deserve the treatment I had endured at the hands of Professor Goliath. I was also convinced without a shadow of doubt that the quality of work I had produced was A+ worthy. Please allow me a brief moment to confess that the professor's name was not Goliath, but it sure felt like I was in battle with a taunting Philistine.

To this day, I still believe the only reason I had finished the class with an A- was because Professor Goliath just did not like me, and quite frankly, at the beginning of the semester, I was not too fond of her either. If you have not figured it out by now, Professor Goliath was really getting under my skin. At the onset of the semester, I literally dreaded going to class. After a few negative experiences with Professor Goliath, I decided to Q-TIP. The moment I decided to quit taking Professor Goliath's actions personally, I changed for the better. I soon realized that God was using Professor Goliath to help me mature spiritually. On numerous accounts, I went out of my way to treat Professor Goliath with kindness, patience, and respect. I did not wait for her to change; I chose to change. Albeit there were times it was obvious that Professor Goliath was being outright disrespectful, I smiled and endured the brunt of her negative actions toward me, but it was not an easy feat. I had even considered reporting her to the dean, but for some odd reason, I chose to forego that approach.

One of the most significant things that had helped me maintain a positive attitude throughout the semester was the fact that my situation was nothing compared to the ridicule and suffering Christ had endured on the cross for my sake. When faced with opposition, Christ *always* responded with love. Consequently, as a born-again believer, I knew that I too had to look beyond Professor Goliath's faults, put aside our differences, and *love her anyway*. When Christ was crucified, He did not take it personally; instead, He cried out, "Father, forgive them, for they do not know what they are doing" (Luke 23:34). Christ saw the bigger picture. He knew that all souls would be lost if He allowed His emotions to get the best of Him. Christ's cry for forgiveness for the very persons who had caused Him great pain was a cry of love, compassion, and forgiveness. Just as our Lord and Savior did not take the actions of His adversaries personally, as women of God, we must model the same. Oftentimes we do quite the contrary, right?

Truthfully, it is not easy to put aside personal feelings when we believe wholeheartedly that we are enduring unwarranted personal attacks. For many of us who can attest to this truth, at some juncture in our lives, most of the personal attacks we have endured have manifested through the form of a broken heart, disappointment, ill treatment, disrespect, subtle shunning, rejection, abuse, neglect, unfair treatment, blocked opportunities, racism, sexism, classism, ageism, or misunderstandings. However, despite these real-life realities, we must Q-TIP and *love anyway*. Why must we Q-TIP and *love anyway*? Because our lives are not our own. Because everything we endure for righteousness' sake brings glory to our Heavenly Father and ultimately liberates us. Of greater significance, every time we view life's harsh blows as an opportunity to glorify God rather than an opportunity to strike back or get even, we are better equipped to see past our pain and disappointments. Even greater, when we Q-TIP and *love anyway*, we are better equipped to forgive others, love unconditionally, and show forth the love of God in the land of the living.

Perchance your Q-TIP challenge calls for you to love someone in a leadership position who has deliberately mistreated you or overlooked you for a promotion you know for certain you deserved. Or maybe it is an acquaintance or, should I say, "a Judas" who is plotting against you and smearing your reputation for no apparent reason. Perhaps it is a close family member, loved one, or friend who has betrayed you. Nonetheless, it does not matter what others have done to you or will do to you; what matters most is how you respond to others' actions toward you. Christ was fully aware that Judas would betray Him, but He loved Judas anyway because He knew that Judas had a purpose for being in His life: to serve as an instrument for God to use to help Christ fulfill His greatest victory, Calvary (John 13:21–30). Everything we experience in life is intended for God's glory. God never intended for our tests and trials to harm us or cause us to become bitter, disgruntled, or cantankerous. Instead, in testing times, God's ultimate plan is to refine us, build up our most holy faith, and strengthen our spiritual muscles for greater victories. Therefore, I encourage you to take joy in knowing that whenever fiery trials or tests exist in your life, there are greater victories on the horizon if your responses in times like these are tendered with love, patience, compassion, and forgiveness. Similarly, remember, "if there is a Goliath in front of you, that means there's a David inside of you." Having said that, the next time you feel as though you are in battle with a taunting Philistine, Q-TIP, love extravagantly, and wait patiently for God to provide the sling and stone to work through you to slay everything that represents a Goliath in your life.

DAILY DEVOTIONAL SCRIPTURES:

◊ Meditate on 1 Corinthians 13 (AMP and MSG versions), 1 Samuel 17:50, John 13:21–30, and Luke 23:34.

LOVE CHARGE:

◊ Whenever you are confronted with circumstances that test your capacity to demonstrate love as God commands, love more, permitting love, patience, kindness, and forgiveness to be your weaponry.

My Sister's Keeper,

Felicia D. Shelton, His Destined Diamond

The Q-TIP Challenge: God Will Provide the Sling and Stone

_____

_____

_____

_____

_____

_____

_____

_____

_____

_____

_____

_____

_____

_____

_____

_____

_____

_____

_____

_____

_____

_____

_____

Biblical Truth no. 19 — Matthew 26:41 (NIV)

THE WATCHING WORLD: CAREFUL REMOVAL OUT OF DARKNESS INTO GOD'S MARVELOUS LIGHT

Watch and pray so that you will not fall into temptation. The spirit is willing, but the flesh is weak.

— MATTHEW 26:41 (NIV)

Beloved Sister in Christ,

On June 23, 2018, twelve boys and their soccer coach were trapped deep inside a dark flooded cave complex in Northern Thailand. The boys and their coach became trapped in the Tham Luang Cave when tumultuous rains flooded the cave and disengaged their escape route. Daily, the media aired this heart-wrenching event across global lines for the watching world to see. After learning of the incident, I watched the nightly news every day and prayed earnestly for the safe rescue of everyone trapped inside the cave. For seventeen consecutive days, darkness inside the cave blocked out any trace of daylight. This reality brought with it grave concerns for medics and the watching world. To begin with, according to physicians, entrapment in darkness for great lengths of time put everyone in the cave at risk of various health issues. Psychological trauma, depression, insomnia, perception distortion, sensitivity to light, and potentially discord amid the cohorts were a few reported health apprehensions the twelve boys and their soccer coach could have conceivably experienced (Geddes, 2018; Theguardian.com, 2018). Even greater, as a consequence of being trapped in darkness for so long, everyone had to be carefully removed from the cave to minimize harsh side effects associated with the absence of exposure to daylight. On July 10, rescue efforts rendered a successful outcome as everyone trapped inside the cave was carefully and safely removed. Sadly, a former Thai navy diver lost his life while taking part in rescue efforts.

From a spiritual perspective, the same spiritual effects ring true when the light of salvation is nonexistent in the lives of men and women. Consequently, unwillingness to accept Christ as one's Lord and Savior, coupled with a lifestyle filled with unrighteous deeds, results in entrapment in spiritual darkness. Any length of time spent in spiritual darkness brings with it grave spiritual risks. Ungodly behaviors, the lust of the eye, unrighteousness, bitterness, resentment, unforgiveness, the sowing of seeds of discord, lying, pride, conceit, jealousy, envy, strife, promiscuity, backbiting, sexual immorality, seduction, and deceit are just a few spiritual risks associated with living in spiritual darkness. Of greater significance, similar to the incident that occurred with the twelve boys and their soccer coach, entrapment in spiritual darkness for great lengths of time requires careful removal out of sin's dark cave. Throughout our journey as believers, we have witnessed a myriad of souls close to us fall prey to sin's diabolical devices. But there is good news. Abba has strategically placed the righteous in the pathway of sinners, not for the righteous to judge, ridicule, condemn, wound, or reject them but to love them unconditionally and pray for their deliverance out of darkness into God's marvelous light so that they too will be set free from the yoke of bondage. Therefore, we must not watch from a distance, nor should we complain about the actions of those around us who are bound by sin; instead, Christ calls us to testify of Him to them, first through demonstrating Christ-like behaviors, and second, through prayer and supplication on their behalves.

Moreover, many of us have experienced the ill effects of sin in the lives of our closest loved ones and acquaintances that have caused us great pain, heartache, frustration, and disappointment. Oftentimes, when we are confronted with these realities, we take it personally and fail to recognize that the culprit at play is the adversary of our faith, not the individual. And so we must Q-TIP and recognize that the adversary's ultimate goal is to kill, steal, and destroy both children of the light and children of darkness. Whenever our loved ones, friends, close acquaintances, or colleagues are entrapped in darkness, despite their actions, we must not succumb to the temptation to strike back or disassociate ourselves from them, even when their actions negatively impact us. Instead, we must love them as Christ loves us, pray for them, and understand with sincere compassion that they are in dire need of deliverance, love, patience, kindness, forgiveness, compassion, prayer, and careful removal out of darkness into God's marvelous light. Of a truth, sin does to the soul what kryptonite does to Superman. Sin is crippling and blinding. One can only see clearly spiritually when Christ is Lord of her or his life.

Perhaps sin has overtaken someone close to you. "How do I know sin is the culprit?" you might ask. "I am not the judge," you might proclaim. While it is not our place to judge others, the Bible clearly states that we will know others by the fruit they bear. "Ye shall know them by their fruits. Do men gather grapes of thorns or figs of thistles? Even so, every good tree bringeth forth good fruit; but a corrupt tree bringeth forth evil fruit. A good tree cannot bring forth evil fruit; neither can a corrupt tree bring forth good fruit. Every tree that bringeth not forth good fruit is hewn down and cast into the fire. Wherefore by their fruits, ye shall know them" (Matthew 7: 16–20). Simply stated, righteous living produces godliness and goodness. Sinful acts produce unrighteousness. If a person's actions and confessions are not indicative of godliness and goodness, then it is safe to say they are acts of sin. Conversely, we have hope in knowing that God "hath made Him to be sin for us, who knew no sin; that we might be made the righteousness of God in Him" (2 Corinthians 5:21, KJV). Praise be to God, for He has made a way of escape out of sin for all!

Perhaps your love walk, faith, or patience is being tested by a wayward child, a not-so-supportive family member, a bitter coworker, a disrespectful store clerk, an offensive associate, or someone who is challenged with telling the truth. Or maybe you are challenged with forgiving someone who has broken your heart, abused you, misled you, taken advantage of you, betrayed you, scandalized your name, treated you unfairly, or blocked an opportunity for you to receive a promotion you rightfully deserved. All the aforementioned actions are directly connected to a life that is not fully surrendered to Christ. Whenever we witness or experience these behaviors from others, unlike the world, we should do more than just watch, wonder, complain, harbor resentment, or strike back; we should pray and model 1 Corinthians 13. As women of God, it is imperative that we pray for the lost, forgive those who have hurt us, love those who despitefully use us (Matthew 5:44), and be kind to those who are rude to us. So today let us join our hearts and prayers together and intercede for everyone God has strategically placed in our lives so that they too will be carefully removed out of darkness into God's marvelous light. Whether their presence impacts us positively or negatively, we must remember that they are not in our lives by happenstance.

Truthfully, God desires to carefully remove those around us who are bound by sin out of the enemy's grip far greater than our desire to be delivered out of hardships imposed on us by their actions. And guess what? God wants us to do more than watch and complain about their sinful behaviors. God has chosen us to be conduits of His love through prayer, encouragement, and kindness. Remember, our petitions of prayer are weapons of deliverance for the lost. It is an oxymoron for us to complain about the very souls we are praying and believing for God to deliver out of sin. Therefore, whatever you do, never not stop caring for them and believing for God to save their souls. Even greater, by faith, God will carefully remove our loved ones, family, friends, acquaintances, and foes who are bound by sin, out of darkness into His marvelous light in due season. But until we see the manifestation of salvation in their lives, we must continue to PUSH (pray until salvation happens).

DAILY DEVOTIONAL SCRIPTURES:

◊ Meditate on 1 Corinthians 13, Matthew 26:40, Matthew 7:16–20, and Matthew 5:44.

LOVE CHARGE:

◊ Pray for God to carefully remove everyone around you out of sin who is entrapped in sin.
◊ Extend love, patience, kindness, forgiveness, and compassion to everyone you greet or meet today.
◊ Pray for everyone you encounter today. Despite who they are or what they have done, God loves them.

My Sister's Keeper,

Felicia D. Shelton, His Destined Diamond

The Watching World: Careful Removal Out of Darkness into God's Marvelous Light

_____

_____

_____

_____

_____

_____

_____

_____

_____

_____

_____

_____

_____

_____

_____

_____

_____

_____

_____

_____

_____

_____

_____

_____

_____

Biblical Truth no. 20 — 1 John 2:9-10 (NIV)

The Heart of a Sister: Strategically Placed

Anyone who loves their brother or sister lives in the light and there is nothing in them to make them stumble.

— 1 John 2:9–10 (NIV)

Greetings, Beloved Sister!

The heart of a sister is filled with love, patience, forgiveness, loyalty, and kindness. Personally, I am a living witness of this truth because of the experiences I have shared over the years with my biological sisters. If you are blessed with biological sisters, as am I, in more cases than not, you too can attest to this truth. The relationship my daughters, Aubrianna and Kiyah, have developed with each other over the years is also a testament of this truth. Having biological sisters is truly a gift from God. God blessed me with three beautiful sisters: Tabitha Michelle, Rometha CaTonya, and Angelita Lanier. We share a lot of similarities, but we are also different in many regards. Despite our differences, however, I genuinely love my sisters and accept them just as God fearfully and wonderfully made them. There is no competition among us, and I have never desired to hurt my sisters or see them suffer in any way. Whether my sisters and I are laughing and having a great time together or having a heated disagreement, my capacity to love them unconditionally has always been an easy feat because *true* love conquers all.

A love that conquers all is the true essence of what it means to have a sister's heart. A sister's heart is filled with unconditional love, acceptance, and compassion. If your relationship with your biological sister or sisters is similar to mine, it does not matter what you endure together; someway and somehow, love, patience, forgiveness, loyalty, and kindness always seem to emerge despite the situation. As my mother made it clear to us during our adolescent years, sisters stick together, protect one another, and care for one another. How much more should we as spiritual sisters model the same? When we love one another in this manner, we live in the light, and there is nothing that can cause us to stumble (1 John 2:9–10). Most of us are familiar with the old cliché that states, "Blood is thicker than water." I am a firm proponent of this statement. However, if blood is thicker than water in the natural sense, how much thicker is the blood of Christ, which bonds us together as spiritual sisters? In all actuality, Christ's blood, which bonds us together spiritually, is far greater than the blood that bonds us together biologically. This does not mean that we abandon our biological sisters or love them less than our spiritual sisters, but just as we love our biological sisters unconditionally, I believe we must also love our spiritual sisters the same.

I have come to realize that it is just as easy for me to love my spiritual sisters as it is for me to love my natural sisters because the heart of a righteous sister is not bound by one's biological makeup, ancestry, or mistakes. The key factor to loving beyond kinship is *choice*. As born-again believers, we must choose to love all sisters of the cross as God commands. In fact, God expects each of us to take on the heart of a spiritual sister for every righteous woman He has placed around us. Because God resides in us and God is love, our love for our spiritual sisters should be evidenced by our willingness to genuinely love them beyond their faults or offenses. Equally, God commands us to love all women despite their pedigrees, social classes, races, ethnicities, sexual orientations, or backgrounds. Make no mistake that the women we encounter on a daily basis are not in our space by coincidence. They have been strategically placed in our lives by God for various purposes. At the end of the day, regardless of whether our daily encounters with our spiritual sisters and women in general are peaches and cream or laden with challenges, God has commissioned us to love them.

As born-again women of God, it is hypocritical of us to say that we love God but despise, mistreat, disrespect, disregard, avoid, or refuse to love our biological and spiritual sisters. Moreover, 1 John 4:20–21 states that if anyone boasts, "I love God," and goes right on hating his brother or sister, thinking nothing of it, he is a liar. "If he won't love the person he can see, how can he love the God he can't see?" (MSG). God's command to love is blunt; loving God includes loving all people. Perchance your relationship with your biological sister(s), spiritual sister(s), or women strategically placed in your path by God is severed, laden with challenges, or causing you great pain. Maybe you have not fully forgiven another sister for hard-pressed experiences you have endured with her throughout the years. Maybe many of the experiences you have shared with another spiritual sister are preventing you from forgiving her. Or maybe you have ill feelings toward her. I encourage you to ask God to help you forgive her. Please know that when we let go of unforgiveness, bitterness, and resentment, we are liberated. In contrast, not forgiving others or holding grudges keeps us captive to the enemy's diabolical plot to enslave us spiritually, mentally, and physically.

Consequently, harboring ill feelings toward others does more harm to the person harboring ill emotions than their offenders because "harboring unforgiveness is like drinking poison and hoping the other person dies" (Margaret Stunt). So today let us be mindful of how we treat, view, and talk about our biological, spiritual, and neighboring sisters. Every woman who has crossed our paths and every woman who will cross our paths has been and will be strategically placed in our lives for various purposes. Even if we never fully understand why, let us aim to love them unconditionally, treat them with love and kindness, and forgive them seventy times seventy if necessary. A powerful life-changing Scripture that bears repeating is Matthew 18:21–22—"Lord, how many times will my brother sin against me and I forgive him and let it go? Up to seven times?' Jesus answered him, 'I say to you, not seven times but seventy times seven" (AMP). Love and forgiveness are not optional in the life of a righteous woman. While loving in this manner at times has the propensity to be extremely challenging, doing so is possible. The more we love others, the more God will live in us and make His love complete in us (1 John 4:12).

DAILY DEVOTIONAL SCRIPTURES:

◊ Meditate on 1 John 4:20–21, Matthew 18:21–22, 1 John 4:12, and 1 John 2:9–10.

LOVE CHARGE:

◊ Smile. God loves you.
◊ Love intentionally, especially your enemies.
◊ Be patient with others and especially kind to your sisters, spiritual sisters, and neighboring sisters; God is not through with them yet, just as He is not through with you.
◊ Remember, as long as we have breath in our lungs, there is *always* hope for the lost to be saved.

My Sister's Keeper,

Felicia D. Shelton, His Destined Diamond

The Heart of a Sister: Strategically Placed

_____

_____

_____

_____

_____

_____

_____

_____

_____

_____

_____

_____

_____

_____

_____

_____

_____

_____

_____

_____

_____

_____

_____

_____

Biblical Truth no. 21 — Romans 14:19 (AMP)

MY SPIRITUAL SISTER: STRENGTH FOR THE JOURNEY AHEAD

So then let us pursue [with enthusiasm] the things which make for peace and the building up of one another [things which lead to spiritual growth].
— ROMANS 14:19 (AMP)

Hello, Be-*you*-tiful!

God has blessed me with an overabundant supply of spiritual sisters. But I have one spiritual sister who is a constant support and positive influence in my life. Without a doubt, God has placed her in my life to show forth *His* love for me and encourage me along life's journey. A spiritual sister, first and foremost, is a woman of God who believes in Christ's crucifixion, death, and resurrection. She is a woman who has accepted Christ as her Lord and Savior. She is part of the spiritual sisterhood because of her love for God and other believers. She is loyal to Christ and faith filled, strives to live according to God's principles and precepts, and is loyal to the covenant and bond of spiritual sisterhood. The spiritual sister I am referring to in this commentary never forgets my birthday. I never have to remind her that my birthday is November 6. Each year, like clockwork, she sends me a gift and birthday card in the mail. I can *always* count on receiving a gift in the mail from her on my birthday or a few days before. And whether she knows it or not, every year, I anxiously anticipate receiving her pleasant surprise in the mail because she *always* gives me gifts I absolutely love.

Together, we have shared some of the best sister talks, fellowships, and laugh-out-loud moments. She always allows me to be true to who I am without judgment or ridicule, and she never pries into my personal affairs or treats me like an outcast. Despite the many flaws I possess, she sees me by the Spirit and always respect me as a woman of worth and value. And yes, I have flaws; God is not through with me or you yet. Of greater importance, in addition to her consistently celebrating my birthday in tangible, heartfelt ways, over the course of three years, daily, she had texted me Bible verses or Bible-related devotionals to encourage me in the Lord. When she first began her evangelistic text ministry, I often wondered why she was so dedicated to texting me Bible-related devotionals, especially since everything in my life was going well—peaches and cream, might I add. It was not until I had faced one of the most difficult times in my life that I realized God was using her to feed me the Word of God to strengthen me for the journey ahead. Not only did she do all the aforementioned niceties, but also, she was there for me when I needed her most. I am certain I would have fainted by now if she had not obeyed God when He instructed her to begin her evangelistic text ministry. To date, she is still a very positive influence in my life. I am so grateful for the gift of love we have shared over the years. Our friendship is truly a testament of God's love, grace, and faithfulness toward me.

God places spiritual sisters in our lives to enhance our quality of life. Occasionally, we might not fully understand their God-ordained missions in our lives, but having spiritual sisters is necessary for our spiritual growth and life enhancement. For years, I prayed for God to bless me with spiritual sisters who would love me unconditionally, treat me with love and respect, and protect our friendship through loyalty and trust. God has truly answered my prayers. I have many spiritual sisters who possess these characteristics and more. Having God-ordained spiritual sisters has made all the difference in my life. Each of my spiritual sisters, in some shape, form, or fashion, has played a vital role in building up my faith in God. I am a living witness that every single small kind gesture of love sown into my life by my spiritual sisters has produced life-changing results. Today I encourage you to do as my spiritual sisters have done for me—be an active spiritual sister to another sister in the Lord. If you have not yet identified a spiritual sister you can trust or extend sisterly support to, ask God to bless you with one; I promise you He will send you more than what you ask for.

Truthfully, God did not intend for us to be islands to ourselves; neither did God intend for us to walk life's journey absent of spiritual sisters. There is an array of women of God who are authentic, trustworthy, considerate, and well able to show forth God's love, righteousness, and glory where-soever they go. Today I encourage you to aim earnestly to build Godly relationships with other righteous women by investing in their spiritual growth and allowing them to invest in yours. All it takes is a few moments to make a *huge* life-altering impact. While you may not know the impact of the seeds of encouragement you sow today, regardless, your sister will benefit significantly. Will you join the fold of spiritual sisters and willingly share sisterly love and support to another sister consistently? Would you take time out of your busy schedule to pray for a sister outside of your immediate family? Would you allow God to use you to strengthen another sister for the journey ahead of her? And would you make a concerted effort today to reach out to another sister to encourage her in the Lord? In all ac-tuality, the seed you sow into another sister's life may not be for her present circumstances but for the journey ahead of her.

DAILY DEVOTIONAL SCRIPTURES:

◊ Meditate on 1 Corinthians 13 (AMP and MSG versions) and Romans 14:19.

LOVE CHARGE:

◊ Seek out a spiritual sister today. Be intentional about establishing a relationship with her. Remember, we are our sister's keepers.
◊ Celebrate a spiritual sister today. A small token of kindness may be the lifeline she needs to hang in there.
◊ Keep peace with your spiritual sisters *always*.
◊ Offer a listening ear to a spiritual sister in need. Just listen. Only provide advice if she asks for it.

My Sister's Keeper,

Felicia D. Shelton, His Destined Diamond

My Spiritual Sister: Strength for the Journey Ahead

_____

_____

_____

_____

_____

_____

_____

_____

_____

_____

_____

_____

_____

_____

_____

_____

_____

_____

_____

_____

_____

_____

_____

_____

_____

_____

_____

A TIME TO PRAY
WITHOUT CEASING

Spiritual refreshing is a lifelong journey. Each day, we must be consistent with spending time in the Word of God, and in prayer. In His presence, we will find spiritual refreshment and become more like Him. As we grow deeper in God, we must also pray for our families, the lost, and one another. Spending time with God is truly the Needful Thing. While we are spending personal time with God, we must also pray that our faith will be renewed, the lost will be saved, and other believers will be strengthened in the Lord.

In Luke 18:1, Christ admonishes the disciples to pray at all times and not to lose heart. Not only is prayer vital, but also, it is equally vital that we do not lose heart or become hopeless and lose the faith. In 1 Thessalonians 5:16–18, it also tells us to "rejoice *always*, pray without ceasing, and give thanks in all circumstances; for this is the will of God in Christ for us!" It is God's will for us to rejoice, pray, and give thanks. When we rejoice, our hearts are encouraged; when we call on God through prayer, He promises to answer us and show us great and mighty things, and when we give thanks to God, we summon Him to inhabit amongst us (Jeremiah 33:3; Psalm 22:3).

One of the main reasons we pray is because we love God and desire to spend time with Him. We also pray because we need God. But greater than these reasons, God wants to hear from us. God longs to spend time with us, and He longs to commune with us. I encourage you to continue to spend time with God in your personal time and talk with Him in prayer because through prayer and spending time with God, we are afforded the privilege to build a stronger, deeper relationship with Him. The ensuing prayers are available to you to incorporate into your time of daily devotion. As you pray these prayers, believe that souls will be saved, lives will be changed for the glory of God, and you will experience deeper levels of refreshing.

BITE-SIZED PRAYERS

The subsequent small, bite-sized prayers, though short in content, are powerful in nature when you make these requests known unto God and believe by faith, without a second thought, that God will hear and answer your prayers.

Help Me to Love as Thou Commands

I understand that I am nothing without love. I fully understand that I cannot say, "I love You, God," whom I have not seen, if I do not love my brother or sister, whom I have seen. I understand that the love I show to other believers signifies my standing as a disciple of Christ. The lack thereof signifies the very opposite. Therefore, God, in the name of Yeshua Hamashiach, help me love unconditionally. Help me not avenge nor hold any grudge against anyone. Help me love my neighbor as I love myself. Help me be patient, kind, long-suffering, and forgiving toward others. And help me love my enemies, everyone who has not given their hearts fully to You, everyone who has betrayed or deceived me, and everyone who has hurt me or persecuted me. In the name of Yeshua Hamashiach, Amen.

A Prayer of Thanksgiving

Father, in the name of Yeshua Hamashiach, I offer praise and thanksgiving to You. Thank you, God, that You have called me to be a fellow worker, joint promoter, and laborer together with and for You. I commit myself to pray and not to faint. I commit myself not to lose heart or give up. I am fearfully and wonderfully made. I confidently and boldly draw near to the throne of grace that I may receive mercy and find grace in times of every need. For this is the confidence that I have in You—that if I ask anything according to Your will, You hear me. Amen.

A Prayer for the Lost

The wage of sin is death, but the gift of God is eternal life in Yeshua Hamashiach, our Savior. Father God, in the name of Yeshua Hamashiach, I lift up my lost family members, friends, and loved ones to You. I lift up my enemies to You, and I ask in the name of Yeshua Hamashiach that You would draw them unto to You, that You would turn their hearts toward You, God, and that You would save them from their sins.

Father God, give them a mind to want to know You and give their hearts fully to You. Let Your presence be known unto them, God. May they feel You surrounding them in this very moment. I ask that You would make them uncomfortable in their sins. Send laborers across their paths to share the message of love and the good news with them. Do not let them rest until they have surrendered their hearts and lives fully to You. Father God, save their souls from darkness, and I pray in the name of Yeshua Hamashiach that You would deliver them from the things that are keeping them from You. Give them a mind to serve You, a mind to love You, and a heart to live for You.

A Prayer of Refreshing

Father God, as I come before Your presence, refresh me. Fill me to the brim with Your peace, love, and joy so that I may pour out the same to those around me. Help me quiet my heart before You as I rest in Your rivers of living waters. Make me new and purify my heart, God. Your Word declares that if I ask, it will be given unto me. Therefore, I ask in Christ's name for You to strengthen me, revive my heart, and refresh my soul.

My Sister's Keeper Prayer

Father, I pray in the name of Yeshua Hamashiach for every woman You have placed in my Circle of influence. Help them to be capable, intelligent, and virtuous women, women filled with faith, diligence, generosity, and spiritual strength. May the language of love and kindness always be in their hearts and on their lips. May they put love into action all the days of their lives. Make them a force of love, light, and goodness to those around them. Bless their deeds, increase their faith, and enlarge their territories.

Father, I cover myself, every woman of faith, and their families with the blood of Christ. Let the fire of God surround and protect our lives from all destruction. Let the angel of the Lord encamp around us and protect us. Cover us with the shadow of Your hand. I pray for the women You will send across my path today. I pray that You would heal them everywhere they have been broken. I decree that every woman in my life is healed, healthy, and whole. I decree that no sickness or disease will plague them because by the stripes Christ bore for them, they are healed. Let Your showers of blessings be upon their lives, God. Bless their end more than their beginning. In Christ's name, Amen.

A Prayer of Confidence and Faith

God, You are my defense and refuge. Lord, You are my shield and hiding place. I find peace and rest in You. No weapon formed against me shall prosper. Every tongue that rises up against me, Thou shall condemn. I am the righteousness of God. Before the world was formed, You chose me to be Your own. I am fearfully and wonderfully made, created in the likeness and image of God. I am a daughter of the Most High King, El Elyon. I am strong and brave; therefore, nothing shall cause me to fear or come against me because God is for me. I am victorious in Christ because You, my God, are fighting for me. I am altogether beautiful in every way. My beauty comes from within me and is precious to You, God.

Honor and strength are my garments; therefore, I can laugh at the days ahead of me. Like a shield, Your loving arms keep me safe and sound. I have faith that can move mountains. I can do *all* things through Christ, who strengthens me. Your plans for me are good and not evil. I know that Thou favors me because You have not allowed the enemy to triumph over me. I have the power within me to decree a thing, and You will bring it to pass. I decree divine healing in my body. I decree abundant blessings, favor, prosperity, and peace over my life, over my family, over my friends, and over every woman of God, in the name of Christ, our King, Amen.

A Prayer for Rest

Father God, I pray for rest. Father, lift every heavy burden I have carried for far too long. Help me rest well and peacefully in You. As I lay before You tonight, grant me a good night's rest. I bind the spirit of worry and anxiety, and I release the spirit of peace and rest over my spirit, mind, and soul. You are the God of peace and rest; therefore, I will rest peacefully in Your presence while I sleep tonight. Let Your angels guard and protect me all the days of my life. And, God, I cast all my anxiety on You, for You care for me. In Christ's name, Amen.

www.ingramcontent.com/pod-product-compliance
Lightning Source LLC
Chambersburg PA
CBHW021652120626
46545CB00002B/830